# STEM *trailblazer* BIOS

# GOPRO
# INVENTOR
## NICK WOODMAN

### MATT DOEDEN

**Lerner Publications**
Minneapolis

Lerner Publications Company
A division of Lerner Publishing Group, Inc.
241 First Avenue North
Minneapolis, MN 55401 USA

For reading levels and more information, look up this title at www.lernerbooks.com.

Content Consultant: Tim Meehan, instructor and consultant in digital arts, and certified paragliding instructor for FlyTim

The Cataloging-in-Publication Data for *GoPro Inventor Nick Woodman* is on file at the Library of Congress.
    ISBN 978-1-4677-5792-8 (lib. bdg. : alk. paper)
    ISBN 978-1-4677-6117-8 (pbk.)
    ISBN 978-1-4677-6281-6 (EB pdf)

Manufactured in the United States of America
1 – PC – 12/31/14

The images in this book are used with the permission of: © iStockphoto.com/EpicStockMedia, p. 4; K.C. Alfred/ZUMA Press/Newscom, pp. 5, 15, 26; © Barry Winiker/Photolibrary/Getty Images, p. 6; © Jim Feliciano/Shutterstock.com, p. 7; © Bloomberg via Getty Images, pp. 9, 16, 18, 25; © iStockphoto.com/Henrik5000, p. 10; © iStockphoto.com/MyfanwyJaneWebb, p. 12; © LatitudeStock/Alamy, p. 13; © Svetlana Sysoeva-Fotolia.com, p. 14; AP Photo/PR NEWSWIRE, p. 19; © EMMANUEL FOUDROT/Reuters/CORBIS, p. 20; © Skip Brown/National Geographic/Getty Images, p. 21; © Denis Poroy/Getty Images, p. 22; © MIKE SEGAR/Reuters/CORBIS, p. 24; Red Bull Stratos/EPA/Newscom, p. 27.

Front Cover: © Bloomberg via Getty Images (camera); Max Morse/Wikimedia Commons (CC BY 2.0).

Main body text set in Adrianna Regular 13/22. Typeface provided by Chank.

# CONTENTS

## CHAPTER 1
**Surfer Boy**      4

## CHAPTER 2
**Finding a Place**      10

## CHAPTER 3
**Making a Splash**      16

## CHAPTER 4
**Looking Forward**      24

Timeline      29
Source Notes      30
Glossary      30
Further Information      31
Index      32

Nick Woodman grew up near the California coast, where surfing is popular. Like this surfer, Woodman enjoyed catching waves.

# SURFER BOY

**P**lenty of technology lovers dream of living in California's Silicon Valley. Nick Woodman didn't have to. He grew up there. Born in 1975, he witnessed the rise of giant tech companies such as Apple and Microsoft. Yet as a boy, Woodman never dreamed of taking the tech world by storm.

Woodman's goal was far simpler. He knew what he wanted to do from the time he was eight years old. He wanted to surf.

The youngest of four children, Woodman was a natural athlete. He played baseball and football in high school. But by the time he was a senior, surfing had become his greatest love. In his free time, he often drove 45 miles (72 kilometers) to the nearest beach. He even started a surfing club at his high school.

Woodman's passion for surfing helped change the world of cameras.

# CHASING WAVES

Woodman was a good student. And he had a knack for technology. When he wasn't surfing, he was building remote-controlled gliders. But when he graduated from high school in 1993, Woodman wasn't planning on a career in technology. He was thinking mostly about his next wave. That's why he wanted to attend the University of California, San Diego (UCSD). It was close to one of the world's best surfing beaches, Black's Beach.

Surfers know Black's Beach for its large and powerful waves.

But UCSD denied Woodman's application. Instead, the University of California, Berkeley, accepted him. Woodman's parents begged him to go there. Berkeley was too far from the beach, though. Woodman was determined to go to UCSD. So he wrote an appeal to the school, explaining why he was a good fit. The university's officials changed their minds. Woodman was in!

San Diego was a perfect spot for him and his surfing classmates. Between classes, he spent as much time as he could at the beach. He hadn't come to UCSD just to ride waves, though. He'd also come to learn.

Woodman started out studying economics. But he didn't enjoy the classes. So he followed his passions. He focused on subjects such as art, writing, and acting. He went on to earn a degree in visual arts.

Woodman also found love while at UCSD. He met a fellow student, Jill Scully. They hit it off, began dating, and eventually married.

## TECH TALK

"In a world where we all try to figure out our place and our purpose here, your passions are one of your most obvious guides. They lead you along life's path . . . to your career."

—Nick Woodman

Woodman pursued a degree in visual arts. He continues to use his creative talents to develop new products.

## Chapter 2

Internet - webpage

http://www...

News ▼        Weather

Favorites

Website

Many new Internet companies were formed in the late 1990s.

# FINDING A PLACE

**W**oodman had big plans after college. He tried to start a website that would sell electronics. His plan was to price every item at two dollars or less. But the business venture failed almost immediately.

Woodman quickly moved on to his next idea. In 1999, he started a company called FunBug. FunBug was a website that combined video games and contests. Users could play games to win cash prizes. This time, Woodman managed to sell his idea to several big **investors**. He and his investors poured almost $4 million into FunBug.

At the time, the Internet was exploding into a big business. Plenty of young tech wizards were striking it rich. All a person seemed to need was a winning idea. Woodman hoped that FunBug was just such an idea.

Unfortunately for Woodman, it wasn't. Part of the problem was timing. Internet companies had thrived in the late 1990s, but many of them collapsed in 2000 and 2001. The crash marked the end of the "dot-com boom." FunBug was one of its many victims.

## DOT-COM BOOM . . . AND BUST

The dot-com boom was a period of rapid growth for Internet-related businesses. In the late 1990s, hundreds of tech companies sprang up. By 2000, many of these companies began to fail. Some companies had poor business plans. Some couldn't compete with similar companies. Only a small fraction of the original dot-com businesses survived past the early 2000s.

A surfer rides a wave in Australia. Woodman was inspired to start a new business during a surfing trip to Australia and Indonesia.

## BACK TO THE BEACH

Twice Woodman had tried to launch his own business. Twice he had failed. He began to question whether he had the skill to succeed.

"I'd never failed at anything before except computer science engineering classes," he said. "So it was like . . . maybe I'm not capable of doing this."

Woodman needed to clear his head. It was time to surf. In 2002, he took a trip to Australia and Indonesia. There, he would ride some of the world's best waves.

Like many surfers, Woodman wanted to capture some of his greatest waves on camera. But he wasn't eager to surf while holding a camera. He wanted the use of both of his hands to stay balanced. And he didn't want to lose his camera at the bottom of the ocean.

Woodman had an idea. He attached a disposable camera to an old wrist strap from a surfboard. Then he wrapped the strap around his wrist. If the strap stayed in place, he'd be able to carry the camera and still keep his hands free. To snap a photo, he'd only need to hold up his arm and press the camera's top button. An instant later, both hands would be free again.

Woodman hit the beach to test out his invention. He paddled out, found his perfect wave, and snapped a picture. It worked! For five months, Woodman put his invention to the test in the waters of the South Pacific. And he started to form a plan.

Disposable cameras are easy to replace if they are broken or lost. These types of cameras were popular in the late 1990s.

## TRY, TRY AGAIN

Woodman returned home energized by his trip. The surfing had helped him refocus on his future. He was ready to improve his invention. The camera strap worked, but it wasn't very secure. The camera tended to flop around loosely on his wrist.

Woodman wanted to upgrade his strap and sell it to other surfers. But first, he needed money. The materials to make the strap were expensive. And Woodman didn't have much savings left.

But Woodman had figured out how to raise some cash. While on his trip, he had bought hundreds of bead-and-seashell belts from a market in Indonesia. He'd bargained the seller

To raise money for his new invention, Woodman and his wife, Jill, sold bead-and-seashell belts like these.

Woodman takes a photo with his wife, Jill, during an alumni event at UCSD. The couple met when they were students at the college.

down to less than two dollars per belt. Then he brought them home. He and Jill loaded up their car and drove up and down the California coast, selling the belts. They sometimes got as much as sixty dollars per belt.

Woodman's family helped out by giving him a **loan**. Finally, Woodman had enough money to start his new business. He called it Woodman Labs. But soon, it would be known by the name of its products: GoPro.

## Chapter 3

Woodman shows off the Hero3+ model. This version was released in 2013.

# MAKING A SPLASH

**W**oodman knew that straps were just the beginning. He needed to create the full package. That included a strap, a camera, and a sturdy casing. At first, Woodman planned to use existing camera models. But he needed something that would hold up in tough conditions. Big-name cameras were too fragile. "I went to all the major camera shows, walking every aisle," he said. "I looked at every booth twice." Yet nothing was a good fit.

Woodman needed a plan B. He found a little-known Chinese manufacturer called Hotax. This company made reusable cameras for snorkelers. Hotax agreed to make cameras for Woodman. And then he was off and running.

Woodman locked himself inside his home and got to work. He often spent eighteen hours a day working with drills, his mother's sewing machine, and other tools. Woodman left nothing to chance. He wore his own strap everywhere, even to bed. He had to know if the strap had any weak points or would make someone sore. And the only way to know was to use it—constantly.

## THE HERO

In 2004, Woodman's system was finally ready to go. He went to an action sports convention in San Diego with his first finished model, the GoPro Hero. This early model included a strap with a 35mm **film** camera. It was a hit. One Japanese buyer ordered one hundred of the gadgets, paying more than $2,000.

From there, Woodman's ideas only got bigger. He wanted to make sure that GoPro was cutting edge. Soon a **digital** camera replaced the film version. Next came a camera that could record short bursts of video.

Woodman holds an original waterproof GoPro camera that used film.

This woman uses a digital GoPro Hero while diving.

GoPro was growing and growing. Woodman hired several college friends—and Jill—as his first employees. But by 2007, Woodman feared he had taken the company as far as he could. He planned to sell control of GoPro to an investment group.

Then in 2008, the world suffered a terrible economic **recession**. The investors who wanted to buy the company lowered their offering price. Woodman refused to sell.

The Hero HD can be mounted on a variety of helmets.

## HI-DEF

GoPro wasn't just for surfers anymore. It had quickly become big in the larger action sports community. In 2009, the company really got athletes' attention. The new Hero HD included a **high-definition** video camera. Anyone—from a race car driver to a skydiver—could record a crystal-clear video of a memorable moment. The Hero HD cost less than most high-quality camcorders too.

The Hero HD was unlike any other camera. It was a smash hit. And that wasn't because of a huge advertising campaign. Much of the success came from word of mouth, especially by social media. Soon athletes were posting their videos to Internet sites such as YouTube.

This photo was captured by a GoPro camera mounted to the front of the paddleboard.

At a 2014 Major League Baseball game, Woodman gets ready to throw out the first pitch. A GoPro camera attached to his cap records the event.

Many of these GoPro videos drew thousands or even millions of views. Athletes tried to post better, more daring videos. Others tried to copy them. And sales soared. Within a year, the Hero HD brought in more than $60 million. Woodman's company had hit the big time.

For Woodman, the experience was amazing. He hadn't expected this level of success. He'd simply worked hard and had fun, as he did with surfing. And as GoPro grew, Woodman kept looking for ways to improve his products. He sensed that the company's journey was only beginning.

# Chapter 4

Starting in 2014, members of the general public could invest in GoPro. Public investments can increase a company's value. Woodman and his team celebrated the day GoPro began taking on public investors.

# LOOKING FORWARD

Woodman had started his company as a way for surfers to take close-up action photos. But GoPro had grown into much more. The company began making mounts that

24

allowed users to put the camera anywhere. Soon the Hero HD had been from outer space to the bottom of the ocean. It was on Hollywood sets and on-site for TV reality shows. One even went deep down into a collapsed mine shaft in Chile!

## THE MAD BILLIONAIRE

The 2008 recession had little effect on Woodman's company. GoPro continued to grow. In 2010, the electronics chain Best Buy began to carry the devices in its stores. Once again, sales soared.

GoPro has developed a wide selection of mounts and straps for cameras.

Woodman *(center)* talks with students after giving a speech in 2014.

In 2012, Woodman got an offer he couldn't refuse. An investment group bought less than 9 percent of his company for a stunning $200 million. Based on that price, GoPro was worth more than $2 billion! A few months later, *Forbes* magazine listed thirty-seven-year-old Woodman as one of the youngest billionaires in the world.

Yet Woodman's great wealth didn't change his passions. He still loved to surf, snowboard, ski, bungee jump, and do other action sports. Some members of the media nicknamed him the Mad Billionaire, due to his extreme hobbies!

Woodman and GoPro continued to draw attention. In 2012, daredevil Felix Baumgartner used one of the company's cameras when he set a record for the highest skydiving jump. A 2014 Super Bowl commercial aired some of the footage. GoPro was rapidly becoming a household name.

## BIG PLANS

Woodman plays hard. But he also works hard. And he's not yet done building GoPro. Recently, he's begun designing cameras that can stream video online in real time. Viewers can watch an event as it happens!

Felix Baumgartner wore a GoPro camera during his record-setting skydive in 2012.

ZENITH

Action sports remain a focus for GoPro. But Woodman and his team are always looking for new customers. Surgeons, law enforcement officers, and scientists are among GoPro's users.

In less than ten years, GoPro went from nothing to the fastest-growing camera company in the United States. Who knows where it could be in another ten years? No matter where it goes, Woodman will likely enjoy the ride.

## TECH TALK

"In surfing terms, there are some waves . . . where you start off easy. But as you go down the line, the wave keeps growing, and the barrel keeps getting bigger and bigger. You keep going faster and faster and faster. When people ask me what it's like [running GoPro], I say it's kind of like that. For my friends and me, this is the best ride of our lives."

—Nick Woodman

# TIMELINE

**1975**

Nicholas Woodman is born in California.

**1993**

Woodman begins attending college at the University of California, San Diego.

**1999**

Woodman starts an Internet game site called FunBug, which soon fails.

**2002**

Woodman founds Woodman Labs, later known as GoPro.

**2004**

Woodman unveils the GoPro Hero, which includes a 35mm still camera.

**2009**

GoPro launches the Hero HD. The brand's popularity explodes.

**2010**

Consumer electronics giant Best Buy begins carrying GoPro models.

**2012**

Woodman sells less than 9 percent of GoPro for $200 million. Felix Baumgartner uses a GoPro camera to film his world record for the highest skydiving jump.

**2013**

*Forbes* declares Woodman one of the world's youngest billionaires.

**2014**

Woodman Labs officially changes its name to GoPro. Felix Baumgartner's GoPro footage from his record-breaking skydiving jump appears in a Super Bowl commercial.

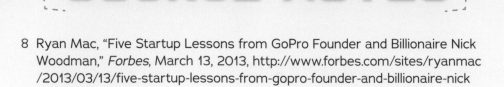

# SOURCE NOTES

8   Ryan Mac, "Five Startup Lessons from GoPro Founder and Billionaire Nick Woodman," *Forbes*, March 13, 2013, http://www.forbes.com/sites/ryanmac /2013/03/13/five-startup-lessons-from-gopro-founder-and-billionaire-nick -woodman.

12  Ryan Mac, "The Mad Billionaire Behind GoPro: The World's Hottest Camera Company," *Forbes*, March 4, 2013, http://www.forbes.com/sites/ryanmac/2013 /03/04/the-mad-billionaire-behind-gopro-the-worlds-hottest-camera-company.

17  Robert Moritz, "Guts, Glory, and Megapixels: The Story of GoPro," *Popular Mechanics*, June 12, 2012, http://www.popularmechanics.com/outdoors /sports/technology/guts-glory-and-megapixels-the-story-of-gopro-8347639.

17  Ibid.

28  Serena Renner, "The Best Ride of Our Lives," *Triton*, accessed May 14, 2014, http://alumni.ucsd.edu/s/1170/emag/emag-interior-2-col .aspx?sid=1170&gid=1&pgid=4381.

# GLOSSARY

**digital**
using or characterized by computer technology

**film**
a light-sensitive medium used to capture images in cameras

**high-definition**
a digital video standard that features a very high degree of detail

**investors**
people or companies that put money into a company or a project in return for a share of the profits later

**loan**
money that is given to someone with the agreement that it will be paid back later

**recession**
a widespread economic downturn

# FURTHER INFORMATION

## BOOKS

Doeden, Matt. *SpaceX and Tesla Motors Engineer Elon Musk*. Minneapolis: Lerner Publications, 2015. Learn about another young tech lover whose business ventures made him a billionaire.

Hubbard, Ben. *Hi-Tech World: Cool Stuff*. New York: Crabtree, 2010. Explore more cutting-edge tech inventions.

Kallen, Stuart A. *Digital Cameras and Camcorders*. Detroit: Lucent Books, 2014. Discover the technology behind cameras such as GoPro.

## WEBSITES

### GoPro
http://gopro.com

The official website for Nick Woodman's camera company shows its latest products.

### How High-Definition Camcorders Work
http://electronics.howstuffworks.com/cameras-photography /digital/high-definition-camcorder.htm

Find out more about how high-tech cameras work.

### YouTube—GoPro
https://www.youtube.com/user/GoProCamera

Check out videos of amazing stunts and faraway places taken with GoPro cameras.

Expand learning beyond the printed book. Download free, complementary educational resources for this book from our website, www.lerneresource.com.

# INDEX

Australia, 12

Baumgartner, Felix, 27

Best Buy, 25

FunBug, 11

GoPro cameras: invention, 13–14, 16–17; strap, 13–14; uses, 20–23, 25, 27. *See also* Hero HD

Hero HD, 20–21, 23, 25

Hotax, 17

Indonesia, 12, 14

Internet, 11, 21

recession, 19, 25

Silicon Valley, 4

sports, 20–23

Super Bowl, 27

surfing, 5–6, 12–14

University of California, Berkeley, 7

University of California, San Diego (UCSD), 6–8

Woodman, Jill (Scully), 8, 15, 19

Woodman Labs, 15

## ABOUT THE AUTHOR

Matt Doeden studied journalism at Mankato State University, where he worked at the college newspaper for three years. Doeden went on to work as a sportswriter for the Mankato paper and then got a job as an editor for a children's book publisher. In 2003, Doeden decided to start his own business as a freelance writer and editor. Since then, he has written and edited hundreds of books on high-interest topics such as cars, sports, and airplanes, as well as curricular topics such as geography, science, and math.